Instrumental Solos for TRUMPET

RODGERS AND HAMMERSTEIN™

How To Use The CD Accompaniment:
A melody cue appears on the right channel only. If your CD player has a balance adjustment,
you can adjust the volume of the melody by turning down the right channel.

ISBN 0-634-02727-1

WILLIAMSON MUSIC®
A RODGERS AND HAMMERSTEIN COMPANY

www.williamsonmusic.com

EXCLUSIVELY DISTRIBUTED BY

HAL•LEONARD® CORPORATION
7777 W. BLUEMOUND RD. P.O. BOX 13819 MILWAUKEE, WI 53213

Visit Hal Leonard Online at
www.halleonard.com

RODGERS AND HAMMERSTEIN™

THE SOUND OF MUSIC®

Contents

◆ DO-RE-MI

TRUMPET

Lyrics by OSCAR HAMMERSTEIN II
Music by RICHARD RODGERS

❷ THE SOUND OF MUSIC

TRUMPET

Lyrics by OSCAR HAMMERSTEIN II
Music by RICHARD RODGERS

❸ MARIA

TRUMPET

Lyrics by OSCAR HAMMERSTEIN II
Music by RICHARD RODGERS

◆ MY FAVORITE THINGS

TRUMPET

Lyrics by OSCAR HAMMERSTEIN II
Music by RICHARD RODGERS

◆5 EDELWEISS

TRUMPET

Lyrics by OSCAR HAMMERSTEIN II
Music by RICHARD RODGERS

rit.

◆ 6 THE LONELY GOATHERD

TRUMPET

Lyrics by OSCAR HAMMERSTEIN II
Music by RICHARD RODGERS

7 SIXTEEN GOING ON SEVENTEEN

TRUMPET

Lyrics by OSCAR HAMMERSTEIN II
Music by RICHARD RODGERS

Relaxed Soft Shoe (♫ = ♩♪)

Piano/Strings

◆8 SO LONG, FAREWELL

TRUMPET

Lyrics by OSCAR HAMMERSTEIN II
Music by RICHARD RODGERS

◆9 CLIMB EV'RY MOUNTAIN

TRUMPET

Lyrics by OSCAR HAMMERSTEIN II
Music by RICHARD RODGERS

PLAY ALONG CD COLLECTIONS

BAND JAM

12 band favorites complete with accompaniment CD, including: Born to Be Wild • Danger Zone • Devil with the Blue Dress • Final Countdown • Get Ready for This • Gonna Make You Sweat (Everybody Dance Now) • I Got You (I Feel Good) • Rock & Roll - Part II (The Hey Song) • Twist and Shout • We Will Rock You • Wild Thing • Y.M.C.A.

_____ 00841232	Flute	$10.95
_____ 00841233	Clarinet	$10.95
_____ 00841234	Alto Sax	$10.95
_____ 00841235	Trumpet	$10.95
_____ 00841236	Horn	$10.95
_____ 00841237	Trombone	$10.95
_____ 00841238	Violin	$10.95

DISNEY SOLOS – INTERMEDIATE LEVEL

An exciting collection of 12 solos with professional orchestral accompaniment on CD. Titles include: Be Our Guest • Can You Feel the Love Tonight • Colors of the Wind • Friend like Me • Under the Sea • You've Got a Friend in Me • Zero to Hero • and more.

_____ 00841404	Flute	$12.95
_____ 00841506	Oboe	$12.95
_____ 00841405	Clarinet/Tenor Sax	$12.95
_____ 00841406	Alto Sax	$12.95
_____ 00841407	Horn	$12.95
_____ 00841408	Trombone	$12.95
_____ 00841409	Trumpet	$12.95
_____ 00841410	Violin	$12.95
_____ 00841411	Viola	$12.95
_____ 00841412	Cello	$12.95
_____ 00841553	Mallet Percussion	$12.95

EASY DISNEY FAVORITES

A fantastic selection of 13 Disney favorites for solo instruments, including: Bibbidi-Bobbidi-Boo • Candle on the Water • Chim Chim Cher-ee • A Dream Is a Wish Your Heart Makes • It's a Small World • Let's Go Fly a Kite • Mickey Mouse March • A Spoonful of Sugar • Supercalifragilisticexpialidocious • Toyland March • Winnie the Pooh • The Work Song • Zip-A-Dee-Doo-Dah. Each book features a play-along CD with complete rhythm section accompaniment.

_____ 00841371	Flute	$10.95
_____ 00841477	Clarinet	$10.95
_____ 00841478	Alto Sax	$10.95
_____ 00841479	Trumpet	$10.95
_____ 00841480	Trombone	$10.95
_____ 00841372	Violin	$10.95
_____ 00841481	Viola	$10.95
_____ 00841482	Cello/Bass	$10.95

FAVORITE MOVIE THEMES

13 themes, including: An American Symphony from *Mr. Holland's Opus* • Braveheart • Chariots of Fire • Forrest Gump – Main Title • Theme from *Jurassic Park* • Mission: Impossible Theme • and more.

_____ 00841166	Flute	$10.95
_____ 00841167	Clarinet	$10.95
_____ 00841169	Alto Sax	$10.95
_____ 00841168	Trumpet/Tenor Sax	$10.95
_____ 00841171	Horn	$10.95
_____ 00841170	Trombone	$10.95
_____ 00841296	Violin	$10.95

HYMNS FOR THE MASTER

15 inspirational favorites, including: All Hail the Power of Jesus' Name • Amazing Grace • Crown Him With Many Crowns • Joyful, Joyful We Adore Thee • This Is My Father's World • When I Survey the Wondrous Cross • and more.

_____ 00841136	Flute	$12.95
_____ 00841137	Clarinet	$12.95
_____ 00841138	Alto Sax	$12.95
_____ 00841139	Trumpet	$12.95
_____ 00841140	Trombone	$12.95
_____ 00841239	Piano Accompaniment (no CD)	$8.95

JAZZ & BLUES

14 songs for solo instruments, complete with a play-along CD. Includes: Bernie's Tune • Cry Me a River • Fever • Fly Me to the Moon • God Bless' the Child • Harlem Nocturne • Moonglow • A Night in Tunisia • One Note Samba • Opus One • Satin Doll • Slightly Out of Tune (Desafinado) • Take the "A" Train • Yardbird Suite.

00841438	Flute	$10.95
00841439	Clarinet	$10.95
00841440	Alto Sax	$10.95
00841441	Trumpet	$10.95
00841442	Tenor Sax	$10.95
00841443	Trombone	$10.95
00841444	Violin	$10.95

MAMBO NO. 5, MARIA MARIA, AND OTHER LATIN HITS

These long-awaited play-along book/CD packs feature 10 super hot Latin hits: Genie in a Bottle • I Need to Know • I Wan'na Be like You (The Monkey Song) • If You Had My Love • Mambo No. 5 (A Little Bit Of...) • Mambo Swing • Maria Maria • Mucho Mambo • Para De Jugar • You Sang to Me.

00841526	Flute	$10.95
00841527	Clarinet	$10.95
00841528	Alto Sax	$10.95
00841529	Tenor Sax	$10.95
00841530	Trumpet	$10.95
00841531	Horn	$10.95
00841532	Trombone	$10.95
00841533	Violin	$10.95

PLAY THE DUKE

Features 11 classics from Duke Ellington's stellar career: Caravan • Don't Get Around Much Anymore • I Got It Bad and That Ain't Good • I'm Beginning to See the Light • In a Sentimental Mood • It Don't Mean a Thing (If It Ain't Got That Swing) • Mood Indigo • Satin Doll • Solitude • Sophisticated Lady • Take the "A" Train.

00841515	Flute	$10.95
00841516	Clarinet	$10.95
00841517	Alto Sax	$10.95
00841518	Tenor Sax	$10.95
00841519	Trumpet	$10.95
00841520	Horn	$10.95
00841521	Trombone	$10.95
00841522	Violin	$10.95

ROCK JAMS

12 rockin' favorites to jam along with the accompanying CD. Songs include: Addicted to Love • Another One Bites the Dust • Get Ready • Love Shack • What I Like About You • and more.

_____ 00841251	Flute	$10.95
_____ 00841252	Clarinet/Tenor Sax	$10.95
_____ 00841253	Alto Sax	$10.95
_____ 00841254	Trumpet	$10.95
_____ 00841257	Horn	$10.95
_____ 00841255	Trombone/Baritone	$10.95
_____ 00841256	Violin	$10.95

FROM

FOR MORE INFORMATION, SEE YOUR LOCAL MUSIC DEALER, OR WRITE TO:

HAL•LEONARD® CORPORATION

7777 W. BLUEMOUND RD. P.O. BOX 13819 MILWAUKEE, WI 53213

http://www.halleonard.com

Prices, contents, and availability subject to change without notice.